INSPIRING STORIES FOR LADIES ON COURAGE

THE LIVES AND LEGACIES OF REMARKABLE WOMEN

NATHANIEL SALLY

The stories and profiles contained in this book are based on the lives and careers of real people and are intended to be accurate and informative. However, some names and details have been changed to protect the privacy of the individuals involved.

INSIDE

As the title suggests, "Inspiring Stories for Ladies on Courage" is a book about the lives of remarkable women who have overcome challenges and achieved great success in their respective fields...

TABLE OF CONTENTS

PREFACE

As the title suggests, "Inspiring Stories for Ladies on Courage" is a book about the lives of remarkable women who have overcome challenges and achieved great success in their respective fields. From scientists like Marie Curie and Eleanor of Aquitaine, to activists like Emmeline Pankhurst and Aung San Suu Kyi, to cultural figures like Rosa Parks and Frida Kahlo, these women have all demonstrated incredible courage, determination, and resilience in the face of adversity.

This book is intended to serve as a source of inspiration and motivation for girls and young women everywhere, and to demonstrate that with hard work, determination, and a willingness to take risks and face challenges head-on, it is possible to achieve great things and make a positive impact in the world. Whether in science, activism, the arts, or any other field, these stories show that with courage and determination, women can overcome any obstacle and achieve great things.

We hope that this book will inspire girls and young women everywhere to pursue their dreams and work towards positive change in the world, and also serve as a reminder of the strength and resilience of women and the power of determination to overcome obstacles and achieve great things.

INTRODUCTION

In this book, we will be exploring the lives of eight incredible women who faced challenges and adversities with bravery and determination. From Malala Yousafzai, who stood up for girls' education in the face of violence and intimidation, to Marie Curie, who broke through barriers in the male-dominated field of science, these women serve as role models for girls everywhere.

Through their stories, we hope to inspire girls to be courageous and pursue their dreams with confidence and resilience. These women show us that no obstacle is too great to overcome and that with courage and perseverance, we can achieve anything we set our minds on.

So join us on this journey of discovery, as we learn about the remarkable lives of these inspiring women and the lessons they have to teach us on courage.

CHAPTER 1

THE STORY OF MALALA YOUSAFZAI

Malala Yousafzai is a Pakistani activist for female education and the youngest Nobel Prize laureate. She is known for human rights advocacy, especially the education of women and children in her native Swat Valley in Khyber Pakhtunkhwa, northwest Pakistan, where the local Taliban had at times banned girls from attending school. Her advocacy has grown into an international movement.

Malala's journey to becoming an advocate for girls' education began when she was just a child. At the age of 11, she began writing a blog for the BBC about life under Taliban rule, using the pseudonym "Gul Makai." In her blog, she described the challenges of living in a society where women were denied basic rights and freedoms, and the importance of education for girls.

In 2012, Malala's activism caught the attention of the Taliban, who targeted her with an assassination attempt. Despite being shot in the head, Malala survived and continued to speak out about the importance of education for girls. She became a global figure and an inspiration to girls around the world.

In 2014, Malala was awarded the Nobel Peace Prize for her efforts to promote girls' education and her activism for human rights. Today, she continues to speak out about the importance of education and the rights of women and girls. Through her courage and determination, Malala has shown that one person can make a difference and inspire change in the world. Malala Yousafzai is a Pakistani human rights activist who is known for her work advocating for the education of girls in her country. She has faced numerous challenges in her efforts to promote education and women's rights, including threats of violence and intimidation.

One of the major challenges that Malala faced was the Taliban's opposition to education for girls in Pakistan. In 2012, the Taliban attempted to assassinate her on her way home from school. Despite being shot in the head, Malala survived the attack and continued her activism.

Another challenge that Malala faced was the cultural and societal barriers that exist in Pakistan toward the education and empowerment of girls. Despite these challenges, Malala has been successful in raising awareness about the importance of education and women's rights in Pakistan and around the world.

Some of Malala's notable achievements include becoming the youngest recipient of the Nobel Peace Prize in 2014 and establishing the Malala Fund, which works to provide education to girls in countries where they are denied access to schooling.

Malala's story is an inspiring example of the resilience and determination of individuals to fight for what they believe in, even in the face of great challenges.
Several lessons can be learned from Malala Yousafzai's case:
The importance of education: Malala's activism highlights the crucial role that education plays in the personal and societal development of individuals and communities.
The power of grassroots activism: Malala's advocacy started at a local level, and through her efforts, she was able to bring about significant change and raise

awareness about important issues on a global scale.

The resilience of the human spirit: Despite facing threats and violence, Malala refused to be silenced and continued to speak out for what she believed in. Her story is a testament to the strength and determination of the human spirit.

The value of standing up for what you believe in Malala's activism serves as an example of the importance of standing up for what you believe in, even in the face of resistance and adversity.

The power of a single individual: Malala's story demonstrates the power of one individual to bring about positive change in the world.

Malala Yousafzai's case highlights the importance of education for women and girls. As a young girl growing up in Pakistan, Malala was denied access to education because of the Taliban's opposition to girls' education. Despite this, she continued to speak out in favor of education for girls and eventually became a global advocate for the right to education.

Through her activism, Malala has brought attention to the plight of girls and women who are denied access to education due to cultural, social, or political barriers. She has also highlighted the positive impact that education can have on the personal and societal development of girls and women.

Malala's case demonstrates the importance of education for women and girls and the need to work towards ensuring that all individuals, regardless of their gender, have access to quality education.

CHAPTER 2

THE STORY OF ROSA PARKS

Rosa Parks was an American civil rights activist who is best known for her role in the Montgomery Bus Boycott. Her refusal to give up her seat on a bus to a white passenger in 1955 sparked a year-long boycott of the Montgomery bus system and played a pivotal role in the American civil rights movement.

Parks was born in Tuskegee, Alabama on February 4, 1913, during a time when segregation and racial discrimination were a daily reality for African Americans. Despite facing numerous challenges and obstacles, Parks became an activist at a young age and was involved in civil rights organizations throughout her life.

As a young woman, Parks attended Alabama State Teachers College (now Alabama State University) where she studied education and political science. After graduation, she worked as a seamstress and a secretary, but she also remained active in civil rights causes. She was a member of the Montgomery NAACP and worked with the organization on voter registration drives and other efforts to challenge segregation and discrimination.

On December 1, 1955, Parks was arrested for refusing to give up her seat on a bus to a white passenger, as was required by the segregation laws of the time. Her act of defiance sparked a boycott of the Montgomery bus system by the African American community, which lasted for over a year and ultimately resulted in the U.S. Supreme Court declaring segregation on public buses unconstitutional.

The boycott was led by a young Baptist minister named Martin Luther King Jr., who would go on to become one of the most important figures in the civil rights movement. Parks and King worked together to organize and mobilize the

African American community in Montgomery, and the boycott became a model for other civil rights campaigns around the country.

Through her bravery and willingness to stand up for her rights, Parks became an iconic figure in the civil rights movement and an inspiration to people around the world. She received numerous awards and honors throughout her life, and her legacy continues to inspire people today. In 2013, President Barack Obama posthumously awarded Parks the Presidential Medal of Freedom, the highest civilian honor in the United States.

Today, Parks is remembered as a symbol of courage and determination in the fight for justice and equality. Her story is an important reminder of the power of individual action and the importance of standing up for what is right, no matter the cost.

Rosa Parks faced numerous challenges and obstacles throughout her life, particularly as an African American woman living in the segregated South during the 20th century. Despite these challenges, she persevered and achieved many successes in her lifetime.

Some of the challenges that Parks faced include:

Segregation: Parks lived in a society where segregation was the norm and African Americans were discriminated against and treated as second-class citizens. She faced segregation in all aspects of life, from education and employment to transportation and public facilities.

Racism: Parks experienced racism firsthand daily, including verbal and physical abuse from white people. She also witnessed the violent mistreatment of other African Americans, including lynchings and other forms of racial violence.

Oppression: Parks faced oppression and discrimination as a woman, particularly in a society where women were expected to adhere to traditional gender roles and were often denied equal opportunities.

Despite these challenges, Parks achieved many successes throughout her life. Some of her notable accomplishments include:

Her role in the Montgomery Bus Boycott: Parks' refusal to give up her seat on a bus to a white passenger sparked a year-long boycott of the Montgomery bus system and played a pivotal role in the American civil rights movement. The boycott was led by Martin Luther King Jr. and became a model for other civil rights campaigns around the country.

Her activism for civil rights: Parks was a member of the Montgomery NAACP and worked with the organization on voter registration drives and other efforts to challenge segregation and discrimination. She also traveled around the country and internationally to speak about civil rights issues and inspire others to take action.

Her awards and honors: Parks received numerous awards and honors throughout her life, including the Presidential Medal of Freedom, the Congressional Gold Medal, and the Martin Luther King Jr. Award for Courage.

Her legacy: Parks' story continues to inspire people around the world, and she is remembered as a symbol of courage and determination in the fight for justice and equality. Her legacy lives on through the work of civil rights organizations and the many people who have been inspired by her story.

CHAPTER 3

THE STORY OF FRIDA KAHLO

Frida Kahlo was a Mexican painter known for her self-portraits and her bold, vibrant style. She is considered one of the most important figures in Mexican art, and her work has been exhibited around the world. Kahlo's paintings often depicted the pain and suffering she experienced in her personal life, as well as the struggles of the Mexican people.

Kahlo was born in Mexico City in 1907. As a child, she was affected by polio, which left her with a lifelong disability. Despite this, she was determined and ambitious, and she excelled in school. In 1922, Kahlo began studying at the National Preparatory School, where she was one of only a few female students.

In 1925, Kahlo was involved in a serious bus accident that left her with multiple fractures and injuries. She was in and out of hospitals for the next three years, undergoing numerous surgeries and treatments. During her recovery, she began painting to pass the time, and she quickly discovered a talent for art.

Kahlo's paintings were often inspired by her personal experiences and struggles. She used her art as a way to express her emotions and confront the challenges she faced in her life. Her paintings often depicted the pain and suffering she experienced as a result of her accident and her disability, as well as the struggles of the Mexican people.

Despite facing numerous challenges and setbacks, Kahlo remained determined and resilient. She continued to paint and exhibit her work, and she became an important figure in the Mexican art scene. She was also active in political causes, supporting the rights of indigenous people and working to promote Mexican culture.

Kahlo's work has been exhibited around the world, and she is considered one of the most important figures in Mexican art. Her paintings are admired for their bold, vibrant style and their ability to capture the human experience powerfully and emotionally. Through her art and her activism, Kahlo has left a lasting legacy and serves as an inspiration to people around the world.

Frida Kahlo faced numerous challenges and setbacks throughout her life, including physical and emotional pain and suffering. Despite these challenges, she achieved many successes and became an important figure in the art world.

Some of the challenges that Kahlo faced included:

Physical disability: Kahlo was affected by polio as a child, which left her with a lifelong disability. She was also involved in a serious bus accident in 1925 that left her with multiple fractures and injuries. She underwent numerous surgeries and treatments as a result of these injuries and experienced chronic pain throughout her life.

Emotional pain: Kahlo's art was often inspired by her personal experiences and struggles, including the pain and suffering she experienced as a result of her physical disabilities and the challenges she faced in her relationships. She used her art as a way to confront and express these emotions.

Political struggles: Kahlo was active in political causes and supported the rights of indigenous people and the promotion of Mexican culture. She faced challenges and opposition as a result of her activism.

Despite these challenges, Kahlo achieved many successes throughout her life. Some of her notable accomplishments include:

Her art: Kahlo's paintings have been exhibited around the world and are admired for their bold, vibrant style and their ability to capture the human experience powerfully and emotionally. She is considered one of the most important figures in Mexican art.

Her activism: Kahlo was active in political causes and worked to support the rights of indigenous people and promote Mexican culture. She made important contributions to these causes through her activism.

Her legacy: Kahlo's work and her story continue to inspire people around the world. She is remembered as a symbol of resilience and determination in the face of adversity.

Overall, Kahlo's life was marked by both challenges and successes. Through her courage and determination, she was able to overcome many obstacles and achieve a lasting legacy as an artist and activist.

Frida Kahlo's life offers several lessons and insights that can inspire and motivate people of all ages. Some possible lessons that can be drawn from Kahlo's life include:

The power of art to express emotions and confront challenges: Kahlo used her art as a way to express her emotions and to confront the pain and suffering she experienced in her personal life. Her paintings demonstrate the power of art to communicate deep and complex emotions and to serve as a form of self-expression and healing.

The importance of resilience and determination: Kahlo faced numerous challenges and setbacks throughout her life, including physical and emotional pain and suffering. Despite these challenges, she remained determined and resilient, continuing to paint and exhibit her work and be active in political causes. Her life serves as a reminder of the importance of persevering in the face of adversity and never giving up on one's dreams.

The value of authenticity and self-expression: Kahlo's art was deeply personal and reflected her own experiences and emotions. She was unapologetic about her authenticity and her willingness to confront difficult and sensitive topics in her work. Her life and art can serve as an inspiration to be true to oneself and to express oneself freely and without fear.

The power of individual action: Kahlo's activism and her willingness to speak out on political issues demonstrate the power of individual action to effect change and make a difference in the world. Her life serves as a reminder of the importance of standing up for what one believes in and working to make a positive impact in the world.

CHAPTER 4

THE STORY OF AUNG SAN SUU KYI

Aung San Suu Kyi is a Burmese politician, diplomat, and Nobel Peace Prize laureate who has been a prominent figure in the struggle for democracy in Burma (also known as Myanmar). She is known for her non-violent resistance to the military dictatorship that ruled Burma for decades, and for her efforts to promote human rights and democracy in her country.

Suu Kyi was born in Rangoon (now Yangon), Burma in 1945. She was the daughter of Aung San, a Burmese independence hero who was assassinated when she was just two years old. Suu Kyi grew up in a political family and was exposed to politics and activism from a young age.

In 1988, Suu Kyi returned to Burma from abroad to care for her ailing mother. Shortly thereafter, a popular uprising against the military dictatorship began, and Suu Kyi became involved in the pro-democracy movement. She quickly emerged as a leader and a symbol of hope for the people of Burma, and she became known for her non-violent resistance to the military government.

Suu Kyi was placed under house arrest in 1989 and spent much of the next two decades in detention. Despite her confinement, she continued to fight for democracy and human rights in Burma and became an international symbol of resistance and courage.

In 1991, Suu Kyi was awarded the Nobel Peace Prize for her efforts to promote democracy and human rights in Burma. After her release from house arrest in 2010, she played a key role in the transition to a civilian government in Burma and was elected to parliament in 2012.

Today, Suu Kyi continues to work for democracy and human rights in Burma, and she remains a powerful and inspiring figure for people around the world. Through her courage and determination, she has demonstrated the power of non-violent resistance and the importance of standing up for one's beliefs.

Aung San Suu Kyi faced numerous challenges and setbacks throughout her life as she worked for democracy and human rights in Burma. Despite these challenges, she achieved many successes and became an international symbol of resistance and courage.

Some of the challenges that Suu Kyi faced include:

Oppression and dictatorship: Suu Kyi lived and worked in a country ruled by a military dictatorship that suppressed basic freedoms and human rights. She faced persecution and detention for her activism and her efforts to promote democracy in Burma.

House arrest: Suu Kyi was placed under house arrest in 1989 and spent much of the next two decades in detention. She was isolated from the outside world and was unable to communicate with her supporters or participate in political life.

Threats and intimidation: Suu Kyi faced numerous threats and intimidation tactics from the military government and its supporters. Despite these threats, she remained committed to her beliefs and continued to fight for democracy and human rights in Burma.

Despite these challenges, Suu Kyi achieved many successes throughout her life. Some of her notable accomplishments include:

Her role in the pro-democracy movement: Suu Kyi emerged as a leader and a symbol of hope for the people of Burma during the 1988 pro-democracy uprising. She became known for her non-violent resistance to the military government and her efforts to promote democracy and human rights in her country.

Her Nobel Peace Prize: Suu Kyi was awarded the Nobel Peace Prize in 1991 for her efforts to promote democracy

Aung San Suu Kyi's life offers several lessons and insights that can inspire and motivate people of all ages. Some possible lessons that can be drawn from Suu Kyi's life include:

The power of nonviolent resistance: Suu Kyi's commitment to non-violent resistance and her ability to mobilize mass movements without resorting to violence demonstrate the power of peaceful protest and the importance of upholding principles of non-violence in the pursuit of justice and change.

The value of courage and determination: Suu Kyi faced numerous challenges and setbacks throughout her life, including persecution and detention. Despite these challenges, she remained determined and courageous, continuing to fight for democracy and human rights in Burma. Her life serves as a reminder of the importance of standing up for what one believes in and never giving up in the face of adversity.

The importance of hope and optimism: Suu Kyi's message of hope and her belief in the possibility of change have been a source of inspiration for the people of Burma and people around the world. Her life serves as a reminder of the importance of holding onto hope and believing in the potential for positive change, even in difficult circumstances.

The power of individual action: Suu Kyi's activism and her willingness to stand up for what she believed in demonstrate the power of individual action to effect change and make a difference in the world. Her life serves as an inspiration to be a force for good and to work to make a difference in the world.

CHAPTER 5

THE STORY OF MARIE CURIE

Marie Curie was a Polish-born scientist who made significant contributions to the fields of physics and chemistry and was the first woman to win a Nobel Prize. She was born Marie Sklodowska in Warsaw, Poland in 1867, and grew up in a family of intellectuals.

Curie showed an early aptitude for science and excelled in her studies. Despite financial challenges and limited opportunities for women in science at the time, she pursued her education with determination and eventually enrolled in the Sorbonne in Paris to study physics and chemistry.

While at the Sorbonne, Curie met her future husband and fellow scientist, Pierre Curie. The two married in 1895 and worked together on several research projects, including the discovery of the elements polonium and radium. These discoveries earned Marie Curie two Nobel Prizes - one in physics in 1903 and one in chemistry in 1911 - making her the first woman to win a Nobel Prize and the first person to win two Nobel Prizes in different fields.

Curie's work revolutionized the field of physics and chemistry and had a lasting impact on scientific research and technological development. She developed new methods for separating and purifying radium and studied its properties, leading to important advances in the understanding of radioactivity.

Curie's work was not without controversy, however. The nature of her research exposed her to high levels of radiation, and she suffered from numerous health problems as a result. Despite these challenges, she continued to work and make important contributions to science until she died in 1934.

Today, Marie Curie is remembered as one of the most important and influential scientists of all time. Her work has had a lasting impact on the scientific community and has inspired countless researchers and innovators around the world.

Marie Curie faced numerous challenges and obstacles throughout her life, particularly as a woman working in the male-dominated field of science in the late 19th and early 20th centuries. Despite these challenges, she achieved many successes and made significant contributions to the fields of physics and chemistry.

Some of the challenges that Curie faced include:

Gender discrimination: Curie faced discrimination and limited opportunities as a woman in the scientific community. She had to overcome numerous barriers and overcome prejudice to pursue her education and career in science.

Financial challenges: Curie and her family faced financial difficulties throughout her life, which made it difficult for her to pursue her education and research. She often had to rely on scholarships and other forms of financial support to afford her studies and her research projects.

Health problems: Curie's work with radium and other radioactive elements exposed her to high levels of radiation, which contributed to several health problems that she experienced throughout her life. These health problems included anemia and aplastic anemia, which ultimately contributed to her death in 1934.

Despite these challenges, Curie achieved many successes throughout her life. Some of her notable accomplishments include:

Her Nobel Prizes: Curie became the first woman to win a Nobel Prize when she was awarded the Nobel Prize in Physics in 1903 for her work on radioactivity. She also won the Nobel Prize in Chemistry in 1911 for her work on radium and polonium, making her the first person to win two Nobel Prizes in different fields.

Her scientific discoveries: Curie made numerous important scientific discoveries throughout her career, including the discovery of the elements polonium and radium. Her work revolutionized the field of physics and chemistry and had a lasting impact on scientific research and technological development.

Her legacy: Curie's work and her story continue to inspire people around the world.

Marie Curie's life offers several lessons and insights that can inspire and motivate people of all ages. Some possible lessons that can be drawn from Curie's life include:

The importance of perseverance and determination: Curie faced numerous challenges and obstacles throughout her life, particularly as a woman working in the male-dominated field of science. Despite these challenges, she remained determined and committed to her work, and she achieved many important successes as a result. Her life serves as a reminder of the importance of perseverance and determination in achieving one's goals.

The value of hard work and dedication: Curie was known for her hard work and her dedication to her research. She spent countless hours in the lab and devoted herself to her work, which ultimately led to her many important discoveries and contributions to science. Her life serves as an inspiration to work hard and to be dedicated to one's pursuits.

The power of education and knowledge: Curie was a lifelong learner who valued education and the pursuit of knowledge. She excelled in her studies and used her education to make important contributions to science. Her life serves as a reminder of the importance of education and the power of knowledge to change the world.

The importance of curiosity and innovation: Curie was known for her curiosity and her willingness to ask questions and challenge the status quo. She was always looking for new ways to explore and understand the world around her, and her innovative approach to science led to many important discoveries. Her life serves as an inspiration to be curious and to embrace innovation and change.

CHAPTER 6

THE STORY OF EMMELINE PANKHURST

Emmeline Pankhurst was a British suffragette who played a key role in the women's suffrage movement in the United Kingdom. She was born Emmeline Goulden in 1858 in Manchester, England, and grew up in a family that was actively involved in social and political activism.

Pankhurst became involved in the women's suffrage movement as a young woman and quickly emerged as a leader and a powerful advocate for women's rights. She founded the Women's Social and Political Union (WSPU) in 1903, and she and her followers became known as the suffragettes. The suffragettes employed many tactics, including civil disobedience and militant action, to draw attention to the cause of women's suffrage.

Pankhurst and the suffragettes faced significant challenges and setbacks as they worked to promote women's suffrage, including persecution, imprisonment, and violence. Despite these challenges, they achieved many important victories, including the passage of the Representation of the People Act in 1918, which granted women over the age of 30 the right to vote in the United Kingdom.

Pankhurst's life and work were marked by her unwavering commitment to the cause of women's suffrage and her willingness to take bold and sometimes controversial actions to bring attention to the issue. She traveled extensively, giving speeches and organizing events to promote the cause, and she faced numerous challenges and setbacks along the way.

Despite these challenges, Pankhurst and the suffragettes achieved many important victories, and their work had a lasting impact on the women's suffrage movement and on the rights of women around the world. Today, Pankhurst is remembered as an important figure in the fight for women's rights and a symbol of courage and determination.

Emmeline Pankhurst and the suffragettes faced numerous challenges and setbacks as they worked to promote women's suffrage in the United Kingdom. Despite these challenges, they achieved many successes and had a lasting impact on the women's suffrage movement and the rights of women around the world.

Some of the challenges that Pankhurst and the suffragettes faced included:

Oppression and discrimination: Pankhurst and the suffragettes lived and worked in a society where women were often denied basic rights and opportunities, including the right to vote. They faced significant discrimination and persecution for their activism on behalf of women's suffrage.

Threats and intimidation: Pankhurst and the suffragettes faced numerous threats and intimidation tactics from those who opposed their activism, including the government and the media. Despite these threats, they remained committed to their cause and continued to fight for women's suffrage.

Imprisonment and violence: Many suffragettes, including Pankhurst, were arrested and imprisoned for their activism. They also faced violence and abuse from those who opposed their efforts.

Emmeline Pankhurst and the suffragettes achieved many important successes in their efforts to promote women's suffrage in the United Kingdom. Some of their notable accomplishments include:

The Representation of the People Act: In 1918, the Representation of the People Act was passed, which granted women over the age of 30 the right to vote in the United Kingdom. This was a major victory for the suffragettes and marked a significant step forward in the fight for women's suffrage.

The Equal Franchise Act: In 1928, the Equal Franchise Act was passed, which granted women the same voting rights as men in the United Kingdom. This was a major victory for the suffragettes and marked the culmination of their efforts to achieve equal voting rights for women.

The influence of their activism: Pankhurst and the suffragettes brought significant attention to the issue of women's suffrage and played a key role in raising awareness and advancing the cause. Their activism inspired other women around the world to fight for their rights and contributed to the broader movement for women's rights and gender equality.

The legacy of their work: Pankhurst and the suffragettes left a lasting legacy and continue to be remembered and celebrated as important figures in the fight for women's rights. Their work has inspired countless people around the world and has had a lasting impact on the rights of women and the broader movement for gender equality.

CHAPTER 7

THE STORY OF JANE GOODALL

Jane Goodall is a world-renowned primatologist, conservationist, and animal rights advocate who has made significant contributions to the fields of anthropology and animal behavior. She is best known for her groundbreaking work with chimpanzees in Tanzania, which has shed light on the intelligence and social behavior of these primates and has contributed to a greater understanding of the natural world.

Goodall was born in 1934 in London, England. She developed a love of animals and the natural world at a young age and spent much of her childhood exploring the forests and fields near her home. She pursued her interests in biology and anthropology as a student, earning a degree in ethology (the study of animal behavior) from the University of Cambridge.

In 1960, Goodall was invited to study chimpanzees in Tanzania's Gombe Stream National Park by paleontologist Louis Leakey. She accepted the offer and began what would become a lifelong study of chimpanzees in the wild. Goodall's work at Gombe revolutionized the study of animal behavior and made significant contributions to our understanding of the intelligence and social behavior of chimpanzees.

In addition to her scientific work, Goodall has also been a vocal advocate for animal rights and conservation. She has worked to raise awareness about the threats facing chimpanzees and other endangered species and has advocated for the protection of their habitats. Goodall has also worked to promote environmental education and sustainability and has founded the Jane Goodall Institute, an organization dedicated to the study and conservation of primates and the promotion of environmental education.

Goodall's work has earned her numerous awards and honors, and she has received numerous honorary degrees and awards for her contributions to science and conservation. Today, she is recognized as one of the world's leading experts on chimpanzees and is a respected and influential voice in the fields of anthropology and animal behavior.

Jane Goodall faced several challenges throughout her career as a primatologist and conservationist. Some of the challenges that she faced included:

Gender discrimination: Goodall faced significant gender discrimination as a woman working in the male-dominated field of science. She encountered resistance and skepticism from some of her male colleagues, who doubted her abilities and questioned the validity of her work.

Limited resources: Goodall often worked with limited resources during her studies at Gombe, and she had to improvise and make do with what was available to her. This often meant working with minimal equipment and supplies, which could be challenging and frustrating at times.

Physical challenges: Goodall's work at Gombe required her to live in remote, rugged conditions and to endure a variety of physical challenges, including extreme heat and cold, mosquitos, and other pests. She also faced physical risks, such as the threat of snakebites and other dangers, which could be stressful and challenging at times.

Political challenges: Goodall's work at Gombe took place in a politically volatile region of Tanzania, and she sometimes had to navigate difficult political situations and confrontations with local authorities and other groups. This could be challenging and potentially dangerous at times.

Despite these challenges, Goodall persevered and achieved many important successes throughout her career. Her work has made significant contributions to the fields of anthropology and animal behavior and has helped to raise awareness about the importance of conservation and the protection of endangered species.

Jane Goodall has achieved many important successes throughout her career as a primatologist, conservationist, and animal rights advocate. Some of her notable accomplishments include:

Groundbreaking research: Goodall's work at Gombe Stream National Park in Tanzania has revolutionized the study of animal behavior and has made significant contributions to our understanding of the intelligence and social behavior of chimpanzees. Her observations and findings have had a lasting impact on the field of anthropology and have been widely cited and influential.

Advocacy for animal rights and conservation: Goodall has been a vocal advocate for animal rights and conservation throughout her career. She has worked to raise awareness about the threats facing chimpanzees and other endangered species and has advocated for the protection of their habitats. Goodall has also worked to promote environmental education and sustainability and has founded the Jane Goodall Institute, an organization dedicated to the study and conservation of primates and the promotion of environmental education.

Honors and awards: Goodall has received numerous awards and honors for her contributions to science and conservation. She has received numerous honorary degrees and has been awarded numerous prizes and awards, including the Presidential Medal of Freedom and the Kyoto Prize.

Influence and legacy: Goodall's work has had a lasting impact on the fields of anthropology and animal behavior and has inspired countless people around the world. She is recognized as one of the world's leading experts on chimpanzees and is a respected and influential voice in the fields of anthropology and animal behavior. Goodall's work and her advocacy for animal rights and conservation will continue to have a lasting impact on the world for years to come.

Jane Goodall's life and work offer several lessons and insights that can inspire and motivate people of all ages. Some possible lessons that can be drawn from Goodall's life include:

The power of curiosity and a love of learning: Goodall's love of animals and the natural world drove her to pursue a career in science and dedicate her life to studying chimpanzees. Her curiosity and her desire to learn and understand more about the world around her have had a lasting impact on the fields of anthropology and animal behavior and have inspired countless people around the world.

The importance of perseverance: Goodall faced many challenges and setbacks throughout her career, but she remained dedicated to her work and persevered in the face of adversity. Her perseverance and determination have been an inspiration to others and have helped her to achieve many important successes.

The power of advocacy and activism: Goodall has been a vocal advocate for animal rights and conservation throughout her career. Her activism has helped to raise awareness about the importance of protecting endangered species and their habitats and has inspired others to take action to protect the natural world.

The value of collaboration and teamwork: Goodall's work has often involved collaboration with other scientists and researchers, and she has demonstrated the value of teamwork in achieving important goals. Her willingness to work with others and her ability to bring people together has been key to her success and have helped to advance the fields of anthropology and animal behavior.

CHAPTER 8

THE STORY OF ELEANOR OF AQUITAINE

Eleanor of Aquitaine was a powerful and influential queen and noblewoman who played a key role in the political and cultural history of Europe in the Middle Ages. She was born in 1122 in the Duchy of Aquitaine, which was located in southwestern France.

Eleanor's father was the Duke of Aquitaine, and she inherited his title and his vast lands when he died in 1137. As the Duchess of Aquitaine, Eleanor was one of the wealthiest and most powerful women in Europe, and she used her position and influence to promote the arts, sciences, and education.

In 1152, Eleanor married Louis VII, the King of France, in a political marriage arranged to strengthen the ties between

Aquitaine and France. Eleanor and Louis had two daughters together, but they divorced in 1152 after 15 years of marriage due to personal differences.

After her divorce from Louis, Eleanor married Henry II, the Duke of Normandy and the future King of England. Henry became king in 1154, and Eleanor served as queen consort of England until she died in 1204. During her time as queen, Eleanor was an influential figure in the English court and played a key role in shaping the policies and direction of the kingdom.

Eleanor's life was marked by a series of significant events and accomplishments, including her role in the Second Crusade, her influence on the English court, and her support for the arts and education. She is remembered as a powerful and influential queen who played a key role in the history of Europe in the Middle Ages.

Eleanor of Aquitaine faced several challenges throughout her life as a powerful and influential queen and noblewoman. Some of the challenges that she faced included:

Political challenges: Eleanor lived in a time of political instability and upheaval, and she had to navigate several difficult political situations during her life. She faced challenges related to her role as queen, including conflicts with her husband and other members of the royal court, and she had to work to maintain her political power and influence.

Personal challenges: Eleanor's life was marked by several personal challenges, including the deaths of many of her children and the failure of her marriages to Louis VII and Henry II. She also had to endure periods of imprisonment and political exile, which were difficult and stressful experiences.

Gender challenges: As a woman in a male-dominated society, Eleanor faced significant challenges related to her gender. She had to work hard to assert her authority and to be taken seriously as a political and cultural figure, and she faced resistance and skepticism from many of her male contemporaries.

Despite these challenges, Eleanor persevered and achieved many important successes throughout her life. She is remembered as a powerful and influential queen and noblewoman who played a key role in the history of Europe in the Middle Ages.

Eleanor of Aquitaine achieved many important successes throughout her life as a powerful and influential queen and noblewoman. Some of her notable accomplishments include:

Inheritance of the Duchy of Aquitaine: Eleanor inherited the Duchy of Aquitaine, one of the wealthiest and most powerful regions in Europe, when her father died in 1137. She used her position and influence as the Duchess of Aquitaine to promote the arts, sciences, and education, and she played a key role in shaping the culture and politics of the region.

Role in the Second Crusade: Eleanor played a significant role in the Second

Crusade, which was launched in response to the fall of the Holy City of Jerusalem to the Muslims in 1187. She traveled to the Holy Land with her husband, Henry II, and provided financial and logistical support to the crusaders.

Influence on the English court: As queen consort of England, Eleanor played a key role in shaping the policies and direction of the kingdom. She was an influential figure in the English court and worked to promote the arts, sciences, and education.

Legacy: Eleanor's life and work have had a lasting impact on the history of Europe in the Middle Ages. She is remembered as a powerful and influential queen and noblewoman who played a key role in shaping the culture and politics of her time.

Eleanor of Aquitaine's life and work offer several lessons and insights that can inspire and motivate people of all ages. Some possible lessons that can be drawn from Eleanor's life include:

The importance of education and the pursuit of knowledge: Eleanor was a strong advocate for education and the arts and worked to promote these values throughout her life. She recognized the value of learning and knowledge and worked to support and encourage the pursuit of these ideals.

The value of leadership and determination: Eleanor was a powerful and influential figure who played a key role in shaping the culture and politics of her time. She demonstrated strong leadership skills and determination throughout her life and was able to achieve many important successes despite facing significant challenges and setbacks.

The power of perseverance: Eleanor faced several difficult personal and political challenges throughout her life, including the deaths of many of her children, the failure of her marriages, and periods of imprisonment and exile. Despite these challenges, she persevered and continued to work towards her goals and achieve important successes.

The importance of collaboration and teamwork: Eleanor's life and work often involved collaboration with others, and she demonstrated the value of teamwork in achieving important goals. She worked with her husband, Henry II, and with other members of the royal court to shape the policies and direction of the kingdom, and she recognized the importance of working together to achieve common goals.

CONCLUSION

The book "Inspiring Stories for Ladies on Courage," tells the stories of several remarkable women who have overcome challenges and achieved great success in their respective fields. From the pioneering work of Marie Curie and Ada Lovelace in science and technology to the activism of Emmeline Pankhurst and Aung San Suu Kyi in the fight for women's rights and political change, these women have demonstrated incredible courage, determination, and resilience in the face of adversity.

Each of these women faced unique challenges in their respective fields and faced obstacles that tested their courage and determination. But they refused to be discouraged by these challenges and worked tirelessly to achieve their goals. Through their hard work and perseverance, they made significant contributions to their fields and left a lasting legacy that continues to inspire and motivate people around the world.

Chapter 1 tells the story of Malala Yousafzai, a Pakistani activist who is best known for her efforts to promote education and women's rights in Pakistan. Yousafzai faced significant challenges and risks in her activism, including a near-fatal assassination attempt, but she persevered and continued to fight for education and women's rights in her country.

Yousafzai's activism has inspired others around the world and has contributed to important changes in Pakistan. She is remembered as a courageous and determined activist and a role model for girls and young women everywhere, and her story serves as an inspiration for others to stand up for what they believe in and work toward positive change in the world.

Chapter 2 tells the story of Rosa Parks, an African American civil rights activist who played a key role in the civil rights movement in the United States. Through her courage, determination, and perseverance, Parks inspired others to join the fight for racial equality and helped to bring about important changes in the United States. Her story is an inspiration for girls and young women everywhere and serves as a reminder of the power of individual action to bring about positive change.

Chapter 3 tells the story of Frida Kahlo, a Mexican painter, and activist who is best known for her self-portraits and her involvement in the Mexican communist party. Kahlo faced significant challenges throughout her life, including a near-fatal bus accident that left her with chronic pain and disabilities, and her tumultuous marriage to the artist Diego Rivera. Despite these challenges, Kahlo persevered and continued to create art and engage in activism throughout her life.

Kahlo's art and activism have had a lasting impact on the art world and political and cultural movements around the world. She is remembered as a pioneering artist and activist who used her art and her platform to promote social justice and equality. Her story is an inspiration for girls and young women everywhere and serves as a reminder of the power of art and activism to bring about positive change in the world.

Chapter 4 tells the story of Aung San Suu Kyi, a Burmese politician, and activist who is best known for her efforts to promote democracy and human rights in Myanmar. Suu Kyi faced significant challenges throughout her career, including periods of detention and house arrest, but she persevered and continued to fight for democracy and human rights in Myanmar.

Suu Kyi's efforts to promote democracy and human rights in Myanmar have inspired others around the world and have contributed to important changes in her country. She is remembered as a courageous and determined activist who has made a significant impact on the political landscape of Myanmar. Her story is an inspiration for girls and young women everywhere and serves as a reminder of the power of individual action to bring about positive change in the world.

Chapter 5 tells the story of Marie Curie, a pioneering scientist who made significant contributions to the fields of physics and chemistry and was the first woman to win a Nobel Prize. Despite facing significant challenges and obstacles as a woman working in a male-dominated field, Curie persevered and achieved many important successes throughout her career. She is remembered as a pioneering scientist and role model for women in science, and her contributions have had a lasting impact on the field of science and our understanding of the natural world.

Through her hard work, determination, and persistence, Curie overcame the challenges she faced and achieved great success in her field. Her story is a powerful reminder of the strength and resilience of women and serves as an inspiration for girls and young women everywhere to pursue their dreams and achieve their goals.

Chapter 6 tells the story of Emmeline Pankhurst, a British suffragette who is best known for her efforts to secure women's right to vote in the United Kingdom. Pankhurst faced significant challenges and risks throughout her career as an activist, including periods of imprisonment and physical abuse, but she persevered and continued to fight for women's rights.

Pankhurst's efforts to secure the right to vote for women in the United Kingdom were instrumental in bringing about important changes in the country, and her activism has inspired others around the world to fight for women's rights and gender equality. She is remembered as a pioneering activist and a role model for women everywhere, and her story serves as an inspiration for girls and young women everywhere to stand up for what they believe in and work toward positive change in the world.

Chapter 7 tells the story of Jane Goodall, a British primatologist and conservationist who is best known for her pioneering work studying chimpanzees in the wild. Goodall faced significant challenges and risks in her work, including working in remote and often dangerous locations, but she persevered and continued to study and advocate for chimpanzees and other animals.

Goodall's work has had a significant impact on our understanding of chimpanzees and other primates and has helped to raise awareness about the importance of conservation and animal welfare. She is remembered as a pioneering scientist and a role model for girls and young women interested in science and conservation, and her story serves as an inspiration for others to follow their passions and work towards positive change in the world.

Chapter 8 tells the story of Eleanor of Aquitaine, the tale of a powerful and influential queen and noblewoman who faced several challenges and achieved many important successes throughout her life. Eleanor inherited the Duchy of Aquitaine, one of the wealthiest and most powerful regions in Europe, and used her position and influence to promote the arts, sciences, and education. She played a key role in the Second Crusade and was an influential figure in the English court as queen consort of England.

Despite facing significant challenges and setbacks, including the deaths of many of her children, the failure of her marriages, and periods of imprisonment and exile, Eleanor persevered and achieved many important successes throughout her life. She is remembered as a powerful and influential queen and noblewoman who played a key role in shaping the culture and politics of her time. Her story is an inspiration for girls and young women everywhere and serves as a reminder of the strength and resilience of women and the power of determination to overcome obstacles and achieve great things.

In conclusion, the book "Inspiring Stories for Ladies on Courage" offers a powerful and inspiring message about the strength, resilience, and determination of women. It is a tribute to the many remarkable women who have overcome challenges and achieved great success in their respective fields and serves as a source of inspiration for girls and young women everywhere.

FURTHER READING

If you are interested in learning more about the inspiring stories of the women featured in "Inspiring Stories for Girls about Courage," there are many additional resources that you might find useful. Here are a few suggestions for further reading:
"Marie Curie: A Life" by Susan Quinn: This biography provides a detailed and engaging account of the life and work of Marie Curie, one of the most influential scientists in history.

"Rosa Parks: My Story" by Rosa Parks: This memoir tells the story of Rosa Parks' life and her role in the civil rights movement, in her own words.

"Frida Kahlo: The Paintings" by Hayden Herrera: This book provides a detailed look at the paintings of Frida Kahlo and offers insight into the life and work of this pioneering artist.

"The Lady: Aung San Suu Kyi, Nobel Peace Laureate" by Peter Popham: This biography tells the story of Aung San Suu Kyi's life and her efforts to promote democracy and human rights in Myanmar.

"Emmeline Pankhurst: A Biography" by June Purvis: This book provides a detailed and comprehensive look at the life and work of Emmeline Pankhurst, a pioneering suffragette, and activist.

"I Am Malala: The Girl Who Stood Up for Education and Was Shot by the Taliban" by Malala Yousafzai: This memoir tells the story of Malala Yousafzai's life and her efforts to promote education and women's rights in Pakistan.

ABOUT THE AUTHOR

As the author of "Inspiring Stories for Girls About Courage," I am thrilled to share this book with you and introduce you to some of the remarkable women who have inspired me throughout my life.

I have always been fascinated by the stories of women who have overcome challenges and achieved great success in their respective fields, and I am passionate about sharing these stories with others. I believe that these stories can serve as sources of inspiration and motivation for girls and young women everywhere and that they can help to demonstrate the incredible strength and resilience of women and the power of determination to overcome obstacles and achieve great things.

Throughout my life, I have been fortunate to meet and work with many amazing women who have inspired me with their courage, determination, and passion for making a positive difference in the world. I hope that this book will help to inspire others in the same way and that it will serve as a reminder of the incredible potential that exists within us all to make a positive impact on the world.

www.ingramcontent.com/pod-product-compliance
Lightning Source LLC
LaVergne TN
LVHW052055160826
845678LV00015B/3249

* 9 7 9 8 3 7 3 6 4 2 6 1 3 *